A Case for Solace

Liz Ahl

LILY POETRY REVIEW BOOKS

Published by Lily Poetry Review Books
223 Winter Street
Whitman, MA 02382

https://lilypoetryreview.blog/

ISBN: 978-1-957755-05-2

Cover art: Landscape with the Fall of Icarus, Pieter Bruegel the Elder
Cover design: Martha McCollough

Contents

1   Attendance

3   About Suffering

4   My Father's Tools

6   Bleeding the House

7   I've Got You Under My Skin

8   Sitting With a Friend

9   Generous

10 Driving Home from a Funeral Service

11 Living in the Shade

12 Tricking the Lilac

13 Suicide Jacket

15 Dear Anthony,

16 Oatmeal

18 Body Language

19 Pool Therapy

20 Etymologies

21 On the Ninth Morning in the Hospital

22 Pre-Existing Condition

23 The Machine You Will Eventually Carry

24 Spurs

25 Mixed Metaphors for Pain Management

26 School for Grieving

27 His Hat

28 Balm

29 Anniversary

30 The End of the Afghan

31 Home Game

32 Good Housekeeping

33 Putting the Flowers Out

34 Chickens

35 When She Comes Home from Camp

36   When the Bread Fails

37   Natural Causes

38   Abide

39   Working Lunch

40   Everything Must Go

41   Blood Brother

42   Shearing

43   Reminder

44   When to Eat the Peach

45   Feast

47   At the 2015 Kennedy Center Honors, Aretha
Drops Her Fur Coat to the Stage

48   Ambush

49   For My Fellow Travelers at the End of the Day-Long Trip

50   On the Annual July 4 Reading of "Song of Myself"

51   Something Good

53   On the Eve of Social Distancing

54   Notes

55   Acknowledgments

A Case for Solace

Attendance

Each class meeting since you died,
I've paused for a moment before
marking you absent, tasting the loss
another time, turning it over
and over against my teeth.

To make no mark at all seems
cowardly, but to mark you present
would be incorrect, except
in a metaphorical sense
I'm still too angry and sad
to entertain.

You're not here, tall, thin stretch of you
folded into the ridiculous desk,
and you'll never be back—
and I've asked myself
as I ticked the box on the roster,
how present were you that last day,
that last class, mere hours before
you gave yourself to the river?

Surely some part of you was already
crossing the parking lot
into the woods, finding a path
to the Pemigewassett,
testing that water.

How absurd, though,
to keep recording your absence,
as if evidence might be needed,
as if such rote accounting
could ever reconcile.

And yet I'm thrown today
when I discover, on the electronic roster,
that you are finally "Deceased,"
the letters of your name
in black now, unlike the other students,
their names still blue and underlined,
meaning their links are live:
I can click on them and go somewhere.

About Suffering

"the sun shone / as it had to..."
           —Auden, "Musée des Beaux Arts"

Two weeks before you went into the river,
my mother found my father kneeling in the pantry,
holding on to a box of cereal, stuck, trembling, not in prayer,
but taken slowly down, humbled to the linoleum by the burst
of the first small stroke. It was a gentle preamble,
a gunshot muffled by goose down. Later at the hospital,
the main event blasted through his body, shut it down
into death, at a stealth that I've decided to call merciful.

Twenty years before you went into the river,
my friend who was about your age leaned into dark waters
of his own, and could not look away, by which I mean
he swallowed a fistful of pills with a handle of gin
to muffle the jagged whispers of despair
that dogged his every waking minute.
But he reached up one last, small time
from inside that hole, and once more was enough.

The afternoon before you went into the river,
we looked at Bruegel's Icarus in class, his thin, pale legs
disappearing into the sea as the fancy ship sails past.
We read Auden's poem, talked about it in the semi-dark.
The delicate bubble of each unanswerable question you posed
floated into the center of the room, strange and mesmerizing;
each one hung, spun slowly, greasing its exquisite circumference
with a thin rainbow before it popped: a tiny splash, then silence.

You went into the river, and time bent and stretched
in all directions, and *went* is the generalization I keep choosing,
its full sail skimming me across a glossy surface. But what about
walked or *jumped*? With the vivid commitments of those verbs
I might make a case for solace. I might stall in deep waters, my sails
slack and useless, my industrious wake calmed. My fear
of both your suffering and my own laid bare in a stillness of witness.
The water of us, in us, all around us. The buoyancy, the drowning.

My Father's Tools

All manner and size of pliers
and clamps and screwdrivers,
some of it recent vintage, some of it
handed down from his own father:

tape measures, T-squares, plastic protractors,
stair gauges, feeler gauges fanned out
like a smudged pewter peacock tail,
each metal feather infinitesimally thinner
than the next;

a dozen hammers
sporting a dozen different heads,
different claws, each tweaked
for its special function,
its unique and preordained purpose.

Every genus of hook and hinge,
of hasp and bracket, I sort
into taxonomic piles,
working down through
the most obscure descendent subspecies.

As I sift through the drawers
and boxes and workbenches and trunks
he left behind for us to empty of their banal
and mysterious contents,
my dead father reminds me:

there is no such thing as a saw—
only hacksaw or band saw or jigsaw or circular saw
and decades of sawdust shorn
from the miniature hulls of ships
onto the cement floor;

no such thing as nail or screw, but
a complex family tree of flooring nail
versus common nail versus masonry nail—
rituals of selection and specialization—
or, as he said, "the right tool for the right job,"
or, as he said, "measure twice, cut once."
There is no such thing as sky
through the window above this worktable—
there is heartscream blue,
there is Neapolitan sunset ripping
a molten seam across the hemisphere

while I am elbow deep
in my father's workshop
sorting tools I don't yet know the names of,
but with a penchant for nomenclature
I inherited from him, its own kind of tool.
There's no such thing as inheritance:
call it winch for the mind,
call it miter-table of naming.

My fingertips are blackened
by hours of handling all this treasure
piece by piece, even the ultimately
unidentifiable creatures still blazing
like totems in my dirty palms—

and there is no such thing as love—
only sawdust and scrap wood
only hacksaw and heartscream
only roofing nails and setscrews
only gauges for measuring, by touch,
the slenderest gaps.

Bleeding the House

An hour since J. left for work and still
I'm heavy in bed, and even the birds
are mostly quiet in the full daybreak—
only an occasional trill escapes the deep woods.
I'm afraid a sadness waits for me downstairs
in the light and the air—hung like damp laundry
between golden floorboards and cloudy skylights—
so I linger upstairs, folding and refolding
actual clothes into dark drawers until
I let myself think maybe the sadness
has departed by now, has lost cohesion
and drained away through the plumbing or followed
an interesting scent up the driveway
to the road. A creature, a ghost, a chemical,
nothing like clean sheets that ask for folding.
But when I come downstairs, it's still there,
it's everywhere, not like laundry, not like
smoke, but more like carbon monoxide,
invisible yet setting off some alarm in me,
and I need to bleed the house of it.
I lift each window, haul open the slider,
seek out another task for my hands,
to ignore or camouflage sadness,
but of course the sadness is today's only chore.

I've Got You Under My Skin

Because the song's so sweet,
and because it's not finished yet,
and because two of us will leave tomorrow
after too short a visit, while you'll stay here
with a headache that never drains away;
because we're home from dinner out
but not ready to swing open these doors,
to step into the next days – and the next –

we linger in the parked car, singing, swaying, snapping,
Nancy and me in the back, you and Dave in the front,
and the cancer, shot through your body and life,
sewn, it seems, into the very seat cushions we sit on.

Between us, not quite one
complete set of lyrics, but we fill the car
with all of our big full daddy-o hearts,
each of us some kind of Sinatra in turn,
singing to what's under our skin:
the thrumming vein of love, the metastatic
groove of love, the last note
we hold for as long and as loud as we can.

Sitting With a Friend

I've come with sandwiches,
chips and drinks, to the house
where his wife died three nights ago,
where he and his daughter held her,
where they listened to the silences
lengthening between each breath
she drew. He asked for a Reuben,
so I brought a Reuben. I didn't know
what chips to get, so brought two kinds.
We sit at the oak kitchen table,
the house strung rafter to sill
with thousands of paper cranes,
and he starts talking, doesn't stop
for two hours, which is how long it takes
for him to eat the sandwich.
Later, he'll go to town hall to see
about death certificates and car titles.
I'll return to the office and inspect
spreadsheets, calculate course enrollments.
Right now, though, I'm visiting my friend
at his old house, or rather, new house,
newly-formed planet with one resident.
The Reuben is my temporary visa,
my password, my rocket ship, the only
currency we might still have in common
in these raw, early days as magma
attempts to assemble itself into landscape.
The seething atmosphere practices
being breathable. We eat together,
me listening, him talking about her,
about Veronica, whose absence
remains uninhabitable.

Generous

At Veronica's party—the one we tried our hardest
to keep from feeling like a memorial service—
the bartender's leisurely pour of whiskey
into my cocktail was so generous, it made me think
he was offering condolences of a kind, and so
I took my drink and walked back to my table,
feeling well-cared for, but then, thinking of Veronica's
generosity, and how what we may remember longest
or most intensely of our gone-away beloveds
is how they made us feel,
                                        it occurs to me:
I am just imagining the generosity of that pour,
in which case Veronica is still with me because I am
generous in my imagining, pouring my imagining
as if it's that bottle of Beam, generous in my assuming,
as she did, the best in folks, in this case
the function room bartender to whom I return
twice more today, infatuated and sorrowful,
tipping gratefully and generously, toasting
and toasting this beautiful world.

Driving Home from a Funeral Service

Each velvet spear of lupine a steeple,
each profusion of lilacs or explosion
of sparrows from the road's edge
laden to sopping with consolation.

I bat them all away like blackflies,
because they, too, want my blood,
like death wants my blood. At last,
a pummeled rabbit carcass, a hymn

of wet fur and snapped bone splayed
on the yellow dividing line,
offers its weird balm.

Living in the Shade

A mile from here, the peonies
have already exploded. Here,
their tiny, tight grenades
only hint at pink, have not yet
blown themselves inside out
though they reach and reach,
bejeweled by shiny black ants,
during the few blazing hours.

A mile down, this road emerges
from the lush throat of maples,
poplars and pines,
and onto the painted asphalt lanes.
The vagrant roadside irises
have already bent and faded,
giving way to succulent spears
of wayward lupine
thrusting up from the ditch.

Here, ferns are just finishing
their unfurling, and the wild raspberries
send their tardy brambles and blooms
into the stingy slice of high noon.

It's a moody dimness, but survivable—
we who live here must forgive
this slowness. We learn a tenderness
towards the moss and fungus,
a reverence for the ephemeral lady slipper,
that eerie orchid, emerging
from the leaf mulch into
the deep pools of cool shade,
far from sunlight's unmediated
and murderous extravagance.

Tricking the Lilac

You must prune away
the dead clusters, the browned
petals that perfumed the air
in moist gusts for a while.

You must persuade the branches
that they don't need to work
so hard on making seeds to spread
from those dead bouquets.

You must offer the lilac a future
of new leaves and blossoms to plan for.
Channel the energies of grieving,
as you must keep the bereaved busy

with the pantomime of living
until it becomes the living.

Suicide Jacket

"… some of these men were wearing suicide jackets."
 – "Militants Attack U.S. Consulate In Pakistan" (NPR, April 5, 2010)

For several days now, you've gone jacketless
in a dazzling, if vague, wash of gratitude
for the generous surprise of unseasonable warmth
painting the hours wall-to-wall
on the heels of a brutal winter.

It is blessedly easy, when the forsythia
is flirting with you full-tilt,
and the robins spend all day in your yard,
to forget to include in your gratitude not merely
the weather and a glass of wine on the deck,
but also the luck of food to eat whenever you want,
the breath you just took, the friend, your work,
a good book to read in an hour that belongs only to you,
and whatever other gifts add up
to not feeling like you must slide your arms
into the silken killing sleeves, and hunt down
an enemy; and whatever other gifts add up
to not being named target or collateral damage
by a bomb-jacketed stranger.

Though sometimes even all the gifts you can count,
and a good share of gratitude for them
are still not warmth enough against the winter
no one else feels. In that sudden, lonely cold,
the glass of wine is like sipping on an incomplete idea of wine;
the books are stupid as bricks; the sunshine
interrogates you but cannot warm you.

You, too, are a stranger. You, too,
have a jacket. Sometimes that jacket,
hanging there on its wooden peg where it always hangs,
looks like the most sensible piece of clothing you own,
despite its rough weave of shrapnel and tripwire.

Other times you're certain there's no way
it could fit you anymore. But always
it is hanging there where you left it, always
it looks a little empty to you; always
there is the possibility of an unseasonably late frost
in which you don't want to get caught.

Dear Anthony,

How much of this world would have been enough?
What map of obscure flavors did so many feasts paint
onto your hopeful, contrarian tongue?
You'd taste anything. You'd go anywhere.
What remote night market dumpling stall
far enough away from whatever sent you seeking?
What regional dialect soothing enough
to cotton your tired ears?
Which grandmother's recipe
for what creature's least
recognizable bones?

Tonight, we're at our small-town American table,
plates laden with cider-braised kohlrabi,
the luck of local pork chops and the last
of last summer's sweet corn from the freezer.
It's all bounty and peace, but we
know enough to know
any night might offer only sawdust,
our taste buds themselves seized by amnesia.

In memory of Anthony Bourdain, 2018

Oatmeal

Jet-lagged, I emerge from the guest room.
From now on, my father's not already up,
not in a pool of light and solitude at the kitchen table,
not nursing a cup of coffee, not skimming the newspaper
he fetched first thing from the end of the driveway.

And so I tend to the once-invisible rituals:
fumble for the wall-switch, turn on the coffee pot,
walk through the salty mist to retrieve the paper.

Later, after the sun steams this damp away,
my mother and brother and I will dip
into the canister of ash with painted ceramic bowls
nobody eats from and, not speaking, scatter
some of his remains around the garden,
saving the rest to pour into Hood Canal.

I put the newspaper on the table.
The coffee beeps that it is finished.
I open the pantry to find boxes of his cereal
untouched after all these weeks;
the mixed nuts, the cans of soup
he sometimes heated for lunch,
the foods he ate but she does not,
an accidental memorial
to the material day-to-day of him.
No funereal platitudes here, just how
the sustenance he took into his body
makes me remember him.

The iconic cardboard cylinder
is a quarter full of the dusty flakes
he'd transform into warm breakfast
with water, a dash of salt, a handful
of walnuts, dried blueberries.
The particular silicone spatula,
the smallest of the saucepans.

The thought of finishing his oatmeal
makes me fear finishing his oatmeal.
On a morning like this, my body
doing what his body used to do,
what else is left
but to click the blue flame awake,
and make myself a bowl.

Body Language

All day long the world
tells my body *no* – the chairs
cross their arms, pretend
I don't exist; the steel corner
of a bathroom stall paper dispenser
stabs my thigh; even the disagreeable
socks emboss lines
into my too-fat leg.

Once I believed
cigarettes loved me
with their endless chain of *yes*,
believed the world did, too,
probably the trick of nicotine's clarity,
like Windex on glass,
along with all those deep breaths
I took on purpose, inhaling
my way through smoke-breaks.

Now my breaths are shallow,
full of a thousand complaints.
Knowing one thing, feeling
another thing, I bruise
through a blur of obstacles
like a bull, nothing
like smoke.

Pool Therapy

At ninety degrees, the pool's *therapeutic*—
like massages are *therapeutic* when gloved
in particular formalities, in particular offices,
and therefore covered by insurance if you've got it.
This pool's not echoing with Marco Polo, not at all
limpid or stimulating or frothing full of sirens
or mermaids. A staircase with two railings descends
into the aquamarine, and I take it step by step,
these ruined knees pressed down by this fat old body until
I'm all the way inside the chlorine-scented bath
and buoyancy's miracle welcomes my angry bones,
soothes them out of friction. The heat coaxes
a kind of release, as if steam could carry off
all that is stuck and stiff and swollen. For half an hour,
I step and bend as commanded, one side to the other,
then a few laps across the deep end, and finally,
back to the stairs. As I emerge, what was borne away
comes slamming back; a physical and *therapeutic* cruelty
I forgot to brace for, steam turning to hot lead,
me somehow heavier than I was when I entered the waters.
Your body is your burden, the air asserts,
and I drag this waterlogged corpse rolled in a carpet
back into the influence of my planet's true gravity,
this old pain with its new name.

Etymologies

The infuser clicks and purrs
over my shoulder, dripping
into my vein precise amounts
of heparin, to keep thin
my murderous blood, which
thickened, shot clotted gobs
up my legs and into my lungs,
filling every space where air
was supposed to go, so that I gasped,
ears ringing, head spinning,
winded as if I'd sprinted.

"Embolism" comes from the Latin,
embolismus: "insertion of days
in a calendar to correct errors,"
an invitation to consider my body
a calendar and my errant blood
a kind of leap day, a rational adjustment.

I've long believed that if I find the name
of everything, I can open the book of it,
seize a sturdy rope of meaning
with me at the end, holding on as if
language weren't the thinnest thread,
an agreement equally liable to dissolve
or break free and travel to my heart
the moment I notice it.

On the Ninth Morning in the Hospital

Two rugged, cheerful x-ray techs arrive with
news that they are *finally here for that hip x-ray!*

No, I say, *not me, I'm not here for my hip.*
Still shielded by their own radiant smiles,

they check the room number – *14? 14!*
This is the room. They are certain.

And for one uncanny moment I suppose
I must be wrong—somehow I'm here for my hip—

but which one? – not my traitorous lungs
or stupid, mutant blood that wants to clot and clot.

But then they realize – *no – aha!* – wrong patient,
wrong room, *so sorry*, they back out, grinning,

"Yeah, you sure don't look like you were born in 1939,"
ha ha, and I'm adrift in some wash between

lingering concern for my hip – but which? –
and a low surge of even fake flattery's reliable balm.

Why yes, thank you, no I am not eighty,
thanks for noticing, ha ha, I'm not that old, no, ha ha—

And then they carry their good news elsewhere,
but my hands remain pressed, one to each hip,

pressed as questions—and my body, warming
beneath them, won't yet venture even

a hesitant answer.

Pre-Existing Condition

I think, therefore I pre-exist.
I pre-exist, therefore I am
carried in the fat sack of this body.

The closer I get to fifty, the more
I ask myself: what's "before?"

I try not to spend too much time
listing, wonder if my doctor's
listening. Paperwork suggests
I exist, I've existed, and maybe
all of this symptom and syndrome
did lurk all along, waiting to bloom
at the joints and in the arteries.

The Machine You Will Eventually Carry

The machine you will eventually carry looks suspiciously like your own body, but it is a briefcase seething with circuits. Breathing with secrets. You will appreciate the red Bakelite handle, the fixtures of brass and calcium. A factory overseas produced the machine you will eventually carry on an assembly line that's long since disassembled. The machine you will eventually carry is very expensive, but please, redeem this coupon. The machine you will eventually carry makes the machine you carry now look sadder than an empty matchbook, but you don't know this yet. The machine you will eventually carry already carries a machine of its own – a little jeweled purse, a faceted whirring of gears and spindles. It will reveal itself soon. It will stoke new impulses. Start listening. In a closet, it waits for you, loyal and monogamous as honeymoon luggage.

Spurs

My kneecaps have spawned
one each, stark, pointed curls

on the x-ray: gray, two ram's horns
for my stubborn bones.

Instead of the smooth purr
of the well-oiled machine,

my scraping joints have made trouble
like two sticks rubbed together make fire.

And so there's a steady, molten burn,
but also the spurring stabs

of a cruel cowboy's heels
I can't outrun.

Mixed Metaphors for Pain Management

As if the blade of it
were an unruly client
or a wedding to plan.

As if pain didn't know
my bones' unlisted
phone number. As if.

Let us put the pain
in a new picture frame
of balsa wood. Let us

book a better venue
for its vise-grip,
its vibrato midnight,

its diva nonsense. Let
the earnest business majors
pitch it with a transient

balm of jargon. As if
it wants to be sold
this bill of goods. As if.

School for Grieving

Some suggested it was my own father's death,
not even three weeks gone, finally catching me,
but even as we sat together, the poetry class
incomplete, in a circle on the grass
in front of the school building,
minutes after the official confirmation,
even as we sat there stunned beneath the tree
you'd climbed just a week or so ago, even as
we sat there, not having class, having instead
that unpoetic silence and those tears, I knew
this grief was its own undisguised creature,
knew what I was tasting
for the first time in the salt of my sorrow
was your own grief, how it insisted
on the river. Years later, I still cross it
twice a day. Even now it will sometimes
slip a bitter spoonful of its silt past my teeth,
down my suddenly tightening throat.

His Hat

Snow salts the brim of my father's hat
which will always be my father's hat
because he inked his name on the line
marked "name" and wrote his phone number
on the line next to the icon of the old-school
black rotary. I wear my father's hat,
which I inherited along with my father's
big head and broad forehead, along with
my father's spotted skin, some of which
needed to be cut out to nip bad
intentions in the bud. His own father lost
most of an ear to the unscreened sun.
If you get close up you can see the tiny white
scar where basal-cell carcinoma was excised
near my own hairline. But it's gray
February, no sun in sight, just low pewter sky
and the whisking of this fine, icy snow
on the stiff brim of my father's hat,
and the missing him settling in like weather.

Balm

Through June's open windows,
its whistle whittled to a screech,
the phoebe scolds, scolds, scolds.
Its raspy, ceaseless question
nests behind my eyes, until

a run of cooler, assonant notes
seeps in with the first sunlight
from the emerald shadows between
pines and newly green poplars:

the hermit thrush pours
its cooling balm across the acres,
keeping pace for an hour
with the pain I'd named *phoebe*;
calming the flare of grief
I'd named *phoebe*.

Anniversary

We've gone Vermonting—me
with my bad knees, and you
with your red pashmina—sampling
all the cheeses, and marveling
at what all's maple-flavored these days.
I've made reservations for fancy dinner
at a place people have heard of.
Both of us are wrong, it turns out,
about what duck confit actually is.
Later, in the king size bed of the motel
that cost less than our bougie arugula,
our braised short ribs, our Linzer torte,
we tuck in and look up "duck confit"
on our devices. We sprawl across
the bed's vast acreage, but I know
we'll wander, in sleep, towards the middle,
end up touching at least, twitching
through the familiar rolodex
of dreams and digestion.

The End of the Afghan

Here you are, having approached the end.
There's still the border to knit,
the border some part of you must have known
you'd reach, even as you drifted through
the comfortable endlessness of the long project.

Here's where you tell yourself about
destinations, but mainly where you dig out
the creased pattern, consult the new set
of coded directions, pick up your needles and pull the tail
of one more skein. You cast on. Cross over.

Home Game

Ten of us crowd around
the feltless dining room table,
chipped up, snacking, chatty,
until a rare tense all-in showdown
shuts us up so well that we hear
the poker-faced neighbors trodding
their second walk of the day
along the gravel road beyond the trees.

Harder to bluff here, among friends,
some for long enough now that we've seen
one another both brilliant and broken.
I split a pot with someone who's seen me weep;
knock close-quartered elbows with others
whose secrets I've stowed carefully:
pocket aces I'll never play.

Good Housekeeping

The ghosts of failed recipes and others
you just now remember you'd planned to try
haunt the corners of this cabinet above the range—
the *herbes de provence* meant
for some stew you were convinced of,
the smoked sea salt, the cardamom pods.

Today, what holds everything together
is a scrupulous cleaning and inventory
of all the dried spices, each of whose names
you must pronounce aloud
as you wipe its tiny jar clean and set it
with the rest spread across the counter
for roll call and inspection.

Each container of dry leaf or powder or seed
is given one shot of fresh air,
one chance to whisper its scent,
to make its case before being returned
to the cool dark cabinet or rejected,
sent out to season the compost
for the midnight diners.

Putting the Flowers Out

Some critter in the shed made
an overwinter nest of the gardening gloves
and so they're chewed and piss-ridden,
and we're in a rush to beat the rain
and to escape the already-swarming mosquitoes,
and we're hungry for lunch,
so we're ungloved, slashing open the bags
of potting soil, dumping them
into the easiest-to-reach pots, pouring
hastily like toddlers sloshing milk
into spilled-over cereal bowls.
We stuff the sweet little begonias
and not-quite-bloomed-yet snapdragons
into the dark mix; cram cock's comb
and coleus, nasturtiums and white clumps of alyssum
into their new mixed families. Our color,
our comfort, our roughly assembled curb appeal,
even as we live in the woods, no curb
from which to view or approve. We water them,
gentle at the end, just as the rain starts.

Chickens

Tonight for dinner, one of the chickens
raised for us over in Bridgewater
by sensible, elder dykes. You helped
process the birds—two days of blade
and blood and feathers, organs
carefully removed; the bucket of feet.

You brought home ten to stow away
in our deep freeze. My job's to roast them up right
so your sweaty slaughter days
are properly paid for. I come to it gratefully,
with lemons and onions, butter and thyme,
a hot oven start before a lower, slower roast.

True, it's not venison brought down
by bow or rifle—we're not the type.
But these drumsticks are still the bones
you brought home to the fire.
I can tell it that way.

When She Comes Home from Camp

My lover wears a layer of dirt
more like a second skin than a shirt,
a layer of sweat-sealed grime earned
from chopping wood,
from evicting a mouse-ridden mattress
from a rarely-used cabin
and scrubbing away the aftermath,
from helping to haul and boil water,
from helping to keep the fire alive
beneath the blaring supermoon.

My lover wears a weekend of skinny dipping
and berry picking, of sharing dinners
cooked by women in the earthen oven
made by women, drinking rum
around the fire fueled by good dry wood
chopped by women. This weekend
of silence and song at the crest of summer
has painted the body I love with earth
and ash and dust, but also it has revealed
a deeper layer, concealed in the day to day:
her wildness unmasked in its happy appetites,
sparkling and strange, a little dangerous.
Some ember pulsing beneath the soot and pitch.
Some name of hers I still don't fully know.

When the Bread Fails

Inside the sweltering farmhouse
the vast kitchen steams inside
the sweltering county,

sweltering July. All the extra wet
finds its way into the chemistry.
When the bread fails, you kick yourself

for not seeing that the bread
would certainly fail. Blame the cook,
blame the kitchen. The salt.

Make croutons for soup
even though it's too hot for soup.
Make do, make light. Call it

monkey butt, knuckle-bone, cracker-scrap.
Break it. Say, *this is my dense and airless
body. Take, eat.*

Natural Causes

You were young, bright beneath
summer's rental tent strung
with white Christmas lights.
We were barefoot, had come to bless
the twenty-first century nuptials,
the wisdom of the married-before.

Ten years later, tagging photos
I never keep up with, there you are.
None of us know where he lives now;
even the most meant promises
of the older and wiser were doomed
to rearrange themselves on a molecular level:
estrangements we were designed
both to suffer and endure.

Abide

—Canon, Georgia

At first I don't notice the thin white braid,
most of it tucked away like contraband
into the well-pressed collar of the old man
waiting in line for peaches in front of me.
Does his wife, snapped-shut purse secured
in the crook of her elbow, insist
on that short-sleeved button-up, starched,
over an undershirt, even in this July heat?
I invent a sternness in her, a shaming;
how she makes him hide his braid because
she can't abide what folks might think of it,
of them, in their town named for Biblical law.

Not until the line starts moving
do I reconsider, allowing that maybe
what his wife can't abide is the thought
of cutting it off, having woven it daily, gently,
smoothed and tied and laid it down
between his shoulder blades for decades now.
Her fingertips against his neck's soft skin,
gathering the plait that won't be seen
by anybody else; her joy alone. Could be
he's even growled at her to "cut it off,"
some morning when he noticed a wince
she couldn't hide, sensed a stiffness
in her braiding hands.

How easily I bound two strangers in a secret
shame; how quickly from the same threads
a more tender tether emerges. Each version
a figment I stitched while waiting for peaches.
A few yards back in line, reader, you might
wonder what I can be trusted to see, to tell.

Working Lunch

To untie the box lunch given to me
was one kind of pleasure: the way
the brown twine tied in a shoelace bow
loosened, but resisted, rubbing against
its own self, hissing against the parchment.
And then another kind of pleasure:
the further noises of everyone else
untying their own rough twine,
unwrapping their crackling paper.

After eating, I saved my twine
and then his twine, and hers, and then
picked up a few lengths abandoned
in the grass beneath the picnic tables.
I tied some together into a loop,
and for a good long time tried to remember
the patterns of pull and turn and hook
and twist. Alone in the shade, I managed
the witch broom first, then unfolded
Jacob's ladder from the creaking ceiling attic hatch
of my own remembering. Muscle memory
freed briefly from a loose tangle.

To play cat's cradle you need a second pair of hands,
so I strung the twine into a rough warp
through the loom of my fingers and held it out
to others, reaching for help. And finally someone
hooked the crossed twine between
his thumbs and forefingers, taking his turn,
then giving me mine. We passed it back and forth
until he held the braided shape I'd started with,
cradle of air and twine and potentially infinite
passing, silent call and response,
handmade together beneath the bright sun.

Everything Must Go

Bring up the damp liquor store boxes
full of insults you swallowed,
and, half-conscious, stored in the basement.
Insults as shiny and cruel
as third-place bowling league trophies,
and you swallowed them all. Drag them
from beneath the stairs out onto the lawn.
What price for the traffic cutoffs,
the taken-for-granteds, the hoard
of sore knuckles and ground-down molars,
a dozen rusting Folgers cans filled to the brim.
Let all the boxes be marked
in earnest block lettering: FREE.
The shelves, clean now, tremble
in their emptiness, daring you
to dismantle them.

Blood Brother

Even when our bodies aren't rent and bleeding,
our chromosomes whisper, *clot, clot, clot.*
Our non-heroic genetic mutation
goads the platelets to huddle up
into random clumps that could cut loose
and kill us where we stand.

So tonight, little brother, I grab
your pale love-handle and jab you with a syringe
meant to thin out the crowds throbbing
deep inside your calf. I've called the cops
to get those drunk, sofa-burning kids off the lawn.
Childless, both of us, in our forties,
and of course you're the first person
I've ever injected with anything.

Hello again, pale splenectomy scar,
trophy of a long-ago skateboarding accident.
Hello midlife midriff. Hello, brother
in mutation. I cast out those manic
delinquents with this magic.
Hello oldest friend, nervous of the needle,
who would do the same for me.

Shearing

A muscled daughter of Maine wrestles
the fat Shetland into position and holds her there
with one arm and between her solid thighs.
With her free hand she wields clippers, buzzing
expertly through the mottled wool,
along every curve, gently unfolding every fold
to make a clean shear. Thousands of sheep
shorn by this woman guide her now,
as she pivots this particular ewe
so that the thick fleece encasing her can be sheared,
nearly in one piece, as with a paring knife
to an apple's skin. The woman has by heart
a complete map of any ewe's body—
the swelling flesh, the tender bone, the thick skin
and the places where the skin thins. Even the ewe's
puffed vulva gets a gentle, perfunctory buzz
while the lambs watch from the adjacent pen,
the little black one bleating and bleating.

Reminder

After an hour in the warm pool
pretending my bad knees could be better,
I'm still achy, pulling on my boots,
worrying into the rest of my day,
when my former student
in the PT room catches my eye
with his movie-star smile.

Even when he was sick or exhausted
or frustrated in my class, which he ended up
having to drop because he smashed up his leg
in his first hockey game of last year's season,
and had to drop most of his classes, endure
half a dozen surgeries and move back home
to recuperate, he smiled.

Months ago when I delivered the card
his classmates signed, he beamed
from his hospital bed, shocking me a little
with his gladness.

And today, wincing as I rise to leave,
I'm glad to see him pulling on his socks after PT
among the more geriatric crowd not fractured
by athletic misadventure. He tells me
his first game back is next Thursday
and we float together in mild awkwardness.

We could be anybody, but today
we're reminded that we are two lucky people
whose ordinary lives stretch beyond
classrooms and offices, beyond ice,
to previously unimagined destinations,
like this scrappy rural PT office,
or wherever we'll bring our bodies next
to do whatever work they demand of us.

When to Eat the Peach

Between unripe and too ripe,
a surprisingly thin sliver—

between taut flesh biting back
and formless surrender,

the slenderest blink.
Tonight, the full strawberry moon

hauls its solstice glow
through the lattice of branches.

If you look away, the sky
might swallow it before

you had a chance to taste the fruit
for the first time in decades.

In the narrowest aperture
a whole world churns borderless

centuries of sweetness for those
who can find a way inside.

Feast

For turning fifty you chose Sorrento, and the cooking class
you hadn't managed on your first visit—

and now, months later, back in your New Hampshire kitchen
you snap the worked dough—just eggs and flour

as you were taught, then feed it through and through
the hand-cranked machine, dialing it thinner each time,

sending it first to Ann at your elbow, then Cathie at Ann's,
then Jeannette and I in turns accept the far edge

of the delicate unfurling. Then to Tabitha, who folds it,
with generous dustings of semolina, folds and folds again,

and then cuts the final uncurling of golden ribbons of *tagliatelle*,
inspired by the hair of Lucrezia d'Este, originally created,

it is said —or joked?— by a nameless court chef,
on the occasion of her marriage to somebody else fancy.

Joke or legend, nobody knows for sure, and tonight
none of us care for any legends save our own, old friends

gathered around the cutting board. Even the best
of our familiar stories grow tired, the woven histories,

all we've loved and listened one another through,
what we've said and what we've kept to ourselves.

I think of the spouses, partners, parents, children
who've left us too soon. But tonight we have dinner—

Ann brought salad, Cathie brought cookies,
Jeannette made blueberry cake. We've got wine

and the last of Tab's beautiful tomatoes. And we have
tagliatelle made by the assembly line of our bodies,

dropped briefly into the salted water, served up
at a table laden with sustenance we all had a hand in.

At the 2015 Kennedy Center Honors, Aretha Drops Her Fur Coat to the Stage

as if it is the whole fallen world sliding
from her shoulders,

as if not even the weight
of the minor seventh chords

can keep her joyful arms
from praising to the rafters

she sprouts wings
from her gilt cap-sleeves

as if she's showing up
the ghost of James Brown

as if that's her president up there
in the balcony catching some spirit

which puny you and I can only
hope to touch as we

dissolve into a pool of gold at her feet
where we belong—

Ambush

I'm plus-one at the buffet-line retirement party
for a judge, the heartfelt speeches, the steak-tips
more tender than you'd expect, the citrus cakes
baked by his clerk, the suited lawyers
and the polo-shirted law enforcement—
all of it, from tributes to plaques, vaguely familiar,
except maybe the county sheriff's
more tender than you'd expect.

The ambush comes when the judge gathers his old friends,
who have brought their instruments, and they launch into
a decent rendition of "Fox on the Run,"
and like a floodlight thrown on behind my eyes,
my dead father fills the room—summoned
by the bluegrass, that plaintive harmonizing,
by the way the fiddler holds his instrument low
in the crook of his elbow, by the banjo player's strange
heavy-metal stance, by the crowd singing along,
by the absence of a harmonica, my father's instrument.
I remember the leather belt dad commissioned to hold
half a dozen HoÜers and one bottle of San Miguel beer.

For My Fellow Travelers at the End of the Day-Long Trip

For the too-tall former baseball pitcher
with the bad shoulder, downing whiskeys
as fast as the flight attendants can **pour** them
on his flight to his father in hospice.

For the chorus of babies at baggage claim,
and for their toddler elders melting down,
having collectively reached the ends of their tiny ropes,
screaming in exhausted call and response.

For the woman who stepped off the curb
and into the slush to pound her small fist against
the dirty side of the last departing greyhound to Portland—
making it stop for the bundled pair fifty yards back,
and for the driver, who stows their luggage
in the salted underbelly.

For the scruffy, too-thin twenty-something
who boarded my bus in Concord, reeking
of fresh, sticky weed, wearing a cloud of it,
possibly transporting a few pounds of it,
who nodded into the tepid light of his cell phone,
spine curled like a man four times his age.

For those who got up early to give us lifts
and for those who wait for us now, in the garish
or spooky terminals, or outside, stomping and pacing
to keep warm in the boring dark
next to the small-town gas station.

I hope I won't forget the way
the glow of that scruffy kid's phone
lit up his sleepy face, showing me
how he always looks
to those who love him best.

On the Annual July 4 Reading of "Song of Myself"

Ashfield, MA

The sun is high and hot. Our heads are bowed
over the loveworn *Leaves of Grass.*
The catbird cries when Whitman's read aloud,

but we don't really mind. Our humble crowd
takes turns by numbered section, more or less.
The sun is high and hot. Some heads are bowed

beneath umbrellas. No one is too proud
to seek the shifting shade when their turn's passed.
I close my eyes when Whitman's read aloud.

I never took communion or kowtowed
in any church as holy or as vast.
The sun is high and hot. Our heads are bowed

against this holiday, against its loud
warmongering, its ordnance and its brass.
I hear no lies when Whitman's read aloud.

We are the patriotic and the proud.
Our circle lobs its yawps across the grass.
The sun is high and hot. Our heads are bowed.
The catbird cries when Whitman's read aloud.

Something Good

Nothing comes from nothing
Nothing ever could
        —Richard Rodgers

In the untended roadside dirt
by the mailbox post, a long stem grows
weeks past the last of the blueberries
I'd wanted to pick more of but missed,
and today—*come see*—a nodding tiger lily,
vivid and shocking, has suddenly unfurled,
the kind of flower one normally plans for
in a carefully choreographed garden bed
or handful of bulbs tucked in before first frost,
and promptly forgotten.

Its garish, hothouse orange, deep brown speckles,
the pistil, the stamen with its lolling filaments—
all unsettle me. By what procreative voodoo
did it come to emerge here, of all places,
a heart blown suddenly open, pressing
the cheeks of its petals to the humid air?

Years ago, you pruned the few blue hydrangea
next to our small house and they didn't return,
and kept on not returning, and we missed them sorely
and joked gently from time to time of our ineptitude—
how we know almost none of the things
we thought one ought to understand as caretakers
of something so large as a house and acres:
pruning, plumbing, the meaning of a sound
from the basement, from inside a wall.

And yet this summer, the neglected hydrangea
bloomed, bounding back unannounced, full
of forgiveness—bygones gone by.

Which is how I find myself
humming that old tune, wondering
if maybe you or I or someone we never met
did something good or right, on purpose
or not, buried a little landmine
of that goodness and wandered off.

On the Eve of Social Distancing

March, 2020

I'm the sole customer at the Route 25 diner,
soaking in the vintage aquamarine and chrome,
the chunky ceramic mug, the quiet.
Here the original Formica's worn,
and the owner tells me how she wouldn't
let them replace it when they bought the place —
shows me the spots where seafoam green's rubbed
away to yellow and brown at the counter's edge —
she demonstrates with her own elbows
where decades of elbows rested on this counter,
as diners straddled these stools, hunched
over bottomless cups of coffee, pot roast, newspaper,
the quiet fellowship of Yankee solitude.

With their skin and sweat they left
these flat curves—the slow increments
of tree rings—not the ones revealed in a cross-section
of felled white pine, but the ones still concealed
by the unbroken bark, still growing
in the wet, living wood.

Notes

"Attendance," "About Suffering," and "School for Grieving" were composed in the wake of the death of Jake Nawn, a student who I was only just beginning to know. I offer them in deepest appreciation of his devoted friends and family, and in honor of the complex ways in which we grieve and remember.

"I've Got You Under My Skin" is in memory of Katherine Sheeder Bonnano and Dave Bonnano.

"Sitting with a Friend" is for Paul Rogalus. "Generous" is in memory of Veronica Rogalus.

"Home Game" is for the usual suspects.

"Feast" is for Scott Coykendall especially, and for Tab, and for so many beloved friends near and far, here and gone, who have fed me in many different ways, and who have let me feed them.

"Reminder" is for Mike Locatelli.

"Blood Brother" is for Andrew Ahl.

"On the Annual July 4 Reading of Song of Myself" is for Jan Freeman.

"On the Eve of Social Distancing" fondly remembers Plain Jane's Diner in Rumney, New Hampshire, where I unknowingly had my last meal inside a restaurant before the March 2020 COVID-19 "lockdown."

Acknowledgments

Big thanks to the editors of the following publications, in whose pages some of these poems first appeared, occasionally in different versions:

Atlanta Review ("About Suffering"), *The Good Men Project* ("My Father's Tools"), *Quartet Journal* ("Living in the Shade"), *River Styx* ("Suicide Jacket"), *Barrelhouse Online* ("Dear Anthony," under the title, "Hunger"), *Rogue Agent* ("Pool Therapy"), *Prairie Schooner* ("His Hat"), *Nimrod International Journal* ("Home Game"), *One Art* ("Good Housekeeping"), *Atticus Review* ("Putting the Flowers Out"), *Good Fat* ("Chickens"), *Lavender Review* ("When She Comes Home From Camp"), *Sliver of Stone* ("When the Bread Fails"), *Able Muse* ("Abide," under the title, "Braid"), *Blast Furnace* ("Everything Must Go," under the title "Rage Sale,"), *Sinister Wisdom* ("Shearing"), *Crab Orchard Review* ("When to Eat the Peach"), *Spiraling/Paris Press* ("At the 2015 Kennedy Center Honors, Aretha Drops Her Fur Coat to the Stage"), *Naugatuck River Review* ("Ambush"), *The Women's Review of Books* ("On the Annual July 4 Reading of Song of Myself"), and *What Rough Beast*/Indolent Books ("On the Eve of Social Distancing").

An earlier version of "Everything Must Go" appeared as "Rage Sale" in the chapbook, *Home Economics*, published in 2016 by Seven Kitchens Press. "On the Annual July 4 Reading of Song of Myself" appeared in the chapbook, *Talking About the Weather*, published in 2012 by Seven Kitchens Press.

Special thank you to Zoë Kay for suggesting, years ago, that *A Case for Solace* might be a good title for the small collection of poems that evolved into this book.

A sabbatical leave from Plymouth State University created space and time for the editing of this manuscript. Thanks to my faculty union, the PSU-AAUP, for fighting to create working conditions in which such labors (of love and otherwise) are made more possible and sustainable. Thanks to the students, faculty and staff at PSU.

Deep gratitude to the Playa Artist Residency Program in Summer Lake, Oregon, where, among a small but mighty group of creative and thoughtful humans, I worked on revisions and edits to this book.

Heartfelt thanks to anybody who has read or listened to my poems and shared your thoughts, questions, applause, recommendations, skeptical eyebrows, laughter, or any other noises of appreciation – thanks for helping me to be a poet. Grace Bauer and Robin Becker – your poems continue to dazzle me and teach me, and your support has meant everything. Ron Mohring, thank you for allowing me to be some small part of the beauty you bring into the world. To Karen McPherson and Ann Hudson: your deep, appreciative critique of earlier versions of this book and of my work generally, across the years, has been transformative. And Jenny JoÚson, thanks for showing me so many things in and around poetry, and perhaps most especially for the notion of the "apophatic." To Ross White and poets on the Grind, thanks for showing up and helping me show up; 33 of the poems in this collection got their start in those daily drafts. To Noah Stetzer, my oldest friend in poetry, every last nickel for you. Deep appreciation to Eileen Cleary, whose compassionate, unsparing attention to these poems has guided me somewhere new, even when I felt certain there was no newness to be had.

To mom, to Andrew, and still to dad, thanks for helping me into and through this world.

To Jeannette, whom I love: thanks for loving me so well through so much.

Liz Ahl is the author of *Beating the Bounds* (Hobblebush Books, 2017), as well as the chapbooks *Home Economics* and *Talking About The Weather* (Seven Kitchens Press), *Luck* (Pecan Grove Press), and *A Thirst That's Partly Mine*, which won the 2007 Slapering Hol Press chapbook prize. Her poems have appeared in numerous literary journals, most recently in *Limp Wrist, Lavender Review, Quartet Literary Journal, Able Muse, Rogue Agent,* and *West Trestle Review.* Her work has also been featured in various anthologies, including *Nasty Women Poets: An Unapologetic Anthology of Subversive Verse, Visiting Bob: Poems Inspired by the Life and Work of Bob Dylan,* and *Show Us Your Papers.* She teaches writing at Plymouth State University and lives in Holderness, New Hampshire.

Printed in the USA
CPSIA information can be obtained
at www.ICGtesting.com
LVHW041353291023
762323LV00008B/976